RAISING GIANT-KILLERS

PARTICIPANT'S GUIDE

RAISING GIANT-KILLERS

PARTICIPANT'S GUIDE

RELEASING YOUR CHILD'S DIVINE DESTINY
through INTENTIONAL PARENTING

BILL JOHNSON
WITH BENI JOHNSON

Chosen
a division of Baker Publishing Group
Minneapolis, Minnesota

© 2019 by BRevived, LLC

Published by Chosen Books
11400 Hampshire Avenue South
Bloomington, Minnesota 55438
www.chosenbooks.com

Chosen Books is a division of
Baker Publishing Group, Grand Rapids, Michigan

Printed in the United States of America

ISBN 978-0-8007-9925-0

Unless otherwise indicated, Scripture quotations are from the New American Standard Bible® (NASB), copyright © 1960, 1962, 1963, 1968, 1971, 1972, 1973, 1975, 1977, 1995 by The Lockman Foundation. Used by permission. www.Lockman.org

Scripture quotations identified NKJV are from the New King James Version®. Copyright © 1982 by Thomas Nelson. Used by permission. All rights reserved.

Scripture quotations identified NLT are from the *Holy Bible*, New Living Translation, copyright © 1996, 2004, 2007, 2013, 2015 by Tyndale House Foundation. Used by permission of Tyndale House Publishers, Inc., Carol Stream, Illinois 60188. All rights reserved.

Scripture quotations identified KJV are from the King James Version of the Bible.

While the daily lessons in this *Participant's Guide* contain the author's insights that follow and complement those in the book, please note that the discussion questions have been prepared for you by Trish Konieczny and the editorial team of Chosen Books to assist you in your group study of *Raising Giant-Killers*.

Cover design by LOOK Design Studio

19 20 21 22 23 24 25   7 6 5 4 3 2

Contents

You Can Raise Giant-Killers

Beni and I wrote *Raising Giant-Killers: Releasing Your Child's Divine Destiny through Intentional Parenting* from our experience raising our own children. We have added this participant's guide to go along with the book so that you, too, can learn to parent with divine purpose and *raise giant-killers who will change the world*.

It is our God-given privilege to raise our children with eternity in mind, and we should all be intentional in our approach to parenting. The goal is to become Kingdom-oriented parents who raise our children with the values of God's Word and who work to build something in them. As parents, we are builders of families, individuals and legacies that last well beyond our own generation. Yes, it costs us something when we build to last, but we pay the price willingly to obtain such a great reward.

Being intentional about parenting does not mean that we will be perfect parents. But then, it does not take perfect parents to raise children correctly. It takes parents who intentionally pursue the values rooted in the Kingdom of God and who do their best, with their Father's help, to pass those values on to their children.

Raising giant-killers for the Kingdom is not reserved for a select few. It is for *you* and your children and your children's children.

Bill Johnson

Invest in Intentional Parenting

How to Use This Curriculum

Ｆ ROM THE EDITORS of Chosen Books: This participant's guide, which is divided into different sessions that follow the chapters you will read in the *Raising Giant-Killers* (RGK) book, is designed to take you through the process of becoming intentional, Kingdom-oriented parents. As you work through these sessions, you will gain a solid scriptural and theological basis for parenting with intention and focus, so that you can help your children reach their divine destiny.

Each session in this participant's guide is divided into four lessons. If you take a day or two to cover each lesson, you can get through each session in about a week, a pace that lends itself well to either individual or small group study. To get the most out of the pages ahead, move through each lesson thoughtfully, taking your time with the readings from the RGK book and any accompanying Scripture readings. After you have read through a lesson and its assigned readings, answer the four "Questions to Consider." As you move through the lessons and answer each question, pray that the Holy Spirit will give you insight and "guide you into all truth" (John 16:13). He is ready to teach you everything you need to know and will fully equip you as parents to carry out His purposes and plans for you and for your children. Keep a ready mind and an open heart, and expect that your heavenly Father will use this study to make you more effective in parenting intentionally and effectively.

At the end of each session, you will also find "Video Takeaways" that recap the highlights from the video segment recorded to go with the session. In the videos, you will find even more insight and teaching about each session's topics. Although the videos are geared for use in a small group setting, you can also watch them individually at home. They are designed to enhance and complement the book and this participant's guide. There is also an eleventh "Question & Answer" bonus video that can be viewed at your small group's final study session or at an optional group wrap-up meeting.

While you can use the RGK book and participant's guide at home to study the topic of raising giant-killers, it would add greatly to your experience to join—or even to host—a small group study so that you and other believers can work through all these materials together. In a small group setting, you can watch the videos and foster in-depth discussion about the readings and questions you are doing. You can also encourage each other as you all grow in your ability to parent intentionally. Within your group meetings, there will be opportunities to relate your parenting experiences to each other and help each other plan for the application at home of all you are learning about raising giant-killers.

If an RGK study group is forming at your church or somewhere nearby, join in. If no study group is available, consider putting one together. To help you do that, a *Raising Giant-Killers Curriculum Kit* is available for group leaders. The kit contains not only the book and participant's guide, but also the video segments and a special *Raising Giant-Killers Leader's Guide* that walks you through the steps to follow in organizing a study group and hosting the individual meetings.

Note that the lessons and questions in this participant's guide are not meant to add to your daily load of tasks to check off your to-do list. We all have enough busywork in our lives. This participant's guide is designed so you can use it with ease. Between session meetings, you can skip one study day and come back the next if needed, or you can do two days at a time. Whatever your schedule, you should be able to get through each session's four daily lessons easily in a week. Each lesson should take only about thirty minutes of your time. Stay faithful in doing the daily lessons, and stick with it from beginning to end. Keep in mind that you will get out of this study what you put into it. The result of your efforts will be well worth the time you invest, and both you and your children will reap the rewards.

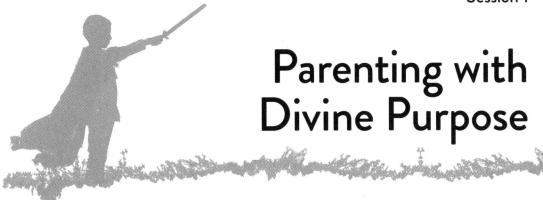

Parenting with Divine Purpose

Stirring up and living with a courageous attitude is what parents and grandparents must do. We have to learn to draw from every biblical example we can find. We must also refuse to be impressed by the size of the giants we face. They are not worthy of the attention. God has already gone before us and set the stage for our triumph through the promises He has given us.

If your answer to prayer is delayed, it is gaining interest. And when breakthrough comes, it will come with greater power and glory than if it had been released at the moment you first prayed. Live with that confidence in all of life. But be certain of doing this with the wonderful privilege of raising *giant-killers*. God designed our children to carry courage into all the earth. They were born for this.

Raising Giant-Killers, chapter 1

Day 1

Positioned for Triumph

The horse is prepared for the day of battle, but victory belongs
to the Lord.

Proverbs 21:31

A s parents, Beni and I were determined to raise our children to
become giant-killers who would change the world. We did not
expect it to be easy. After all, we are all born into a war. But we
did expect that as we stayed faithful to parenting intentionally and with
divine purpose, we would be positioned for triumph. Because Jesus was
victorious on our behalf, we always knew that we were fighting *from*
victory. Not *for* it.

As I say in chapter 1 of *Raising Giant-Killers* (RGK), hope in the victorious Christ is what fuels the home of every family that lives under
the influence of the Spirit of God. It is what fueled Beni and me as we
faced the great privilege and sobering responsibility of raising our children with eternal significance. Each of our children, and now each of
our grandchildren, is a gift from God. So are yours. How we steward
these treasures brings spiritual dividends that reach far beyond our own
homes, into multiple generations of giant-killers yet to be born who will
alter the course of world history.

- Today's Scripture reading: Psalm 127; Romans 5:12–19
- Today's reading from *Raising Giant-Killers*: the introduction and
  the first half of chapter 1 through the "Our Struggle" section

Questions to Consider

1. Bill states in the book's introduction that he and Beni enjoyed each season of their children's lives more than the previous one, without being influenced by the negativity found in the normal home. Who or what are the top two or three influences on your attitude toward parenting? Are they helping you anticipate and enjoy your children's growing seasons, rather than tending you toward "normal"?

   _____

   _____

   _____

   _____

2. Think about how Psalm 127 compares children to arrows in the hands of a warrior. Why is it that parents who raise their children with eternal purpose can have such a great measure of confidence in facing spiritual warfare?

   _____

   _____

   _____

   _____

3. Because of Jesus, we are to reign in life (see Romans 5:17). What does reigning in life mean to you in regard to parenting? In what way do you hope this study will help you achieve that?

   _____

   _____

   _____

   _____

4. In today's RGK reading, Bill makes the statement that the greatest news about true spiritual warfare is that it is not devil focused. What is its focus, and how do our greatest victories come out of that?

   _____

   _____

   _____

   _____

Day 2

A Lifestyle of Courage

For the battle is the LORD's and He will give you into our hands.

1 Samuel 17:47

How do you view your ability to raise children? Are you more aware of your inability, or of God's ability to help you? As you face those important questions in today's lesson, keep in mind one of the most vital Kingdom principles: *God enables what He promises.*

It takes a lifestyle of courage to walk out our faith in that principle, particularly in the area of intentional parenting. But when we stand on that principle, it gives us the courage to face and destroy our own giants. When we do that, our example of living a lifestyle of courage becomes our children's inheritance.

As we see in today's readings, David had that kind of courage. Caleb and Joshua had that kind of courage. And as a parent raising giant-killers, you can and must have that kind of courage, too.

- Today's Scripture reading: Joshua 14:6–15; 1 Samuel 17:45–51
- Today's reading from *Raising Giant-Killers*: the second half of chapter 1, starting at "A Shepherd Boy"

Questions to Consider

1. When David went up against Goliath as a young shepherd boy, in what way was he confronting Israel's history of fearing giants? What does this show you about how God designed our children to carry courage into all the earth?

2. From today's RGK reading, what is the difference between self-confidence and God confidence? How will thinking about this difference alter your approach to parenting?

3. What effect does it have on you as a parent to realize that children do not receive some sort of junior Holy Ghost?

4. As Bill said in today's RGK reading, the greatest contribution we can make to our children's level of courage is to introduce them to a heavenly Father who is moved by their heart's cry. In what way is this the source of extraordinary courage for them?

Day 3

Living beyond Normal

Didn't the LORD make you one . . .? In body and spirit you are his. And what does he want? Godly children from your union.

Malachi 2:15 NLT

YOU MAY HAVE HAD godly, Kingdom-oriented parents who raised you with eternity in mind. Or you may have had parents who just did the best they could to meet your needs and survive their parenting years. You may even have had worldly parents who raised you in what could only be called a hellish environment. Any of these could have influenced the way you have parented your children up to this point. But from now on, we are all on equal footing. Regardless of our background, we all have a heavenly Father who is the ultimate parent to us.

When we know the Father, it raises us as parents. The best among us are perfectly imperfect, but He is perfect, generous, kind and loving, so from this point forward we have no more excuses. We can learn what our Father is like as a parent and do our best to become like Him.

The way we live in unity as a husband and a wife, raising children together in our home, is meant to model "on earth as it is in heaven." Even a single-parent home, through God's grace, can model this to the world. In fact, as we see in today's lesson, it is His grace and enablement that make it possible at all for any of us to raise giant-killers.

- Today's Scripture reading: Ephesians 5:22–33
- Today's reading from *Raising Giant-Killers*: the first half of chapter 2, through "The Ideal and the Reality" section

Questions to Consider

1. It does not take perfect parents from healthy backgrounds to raise children correctly. What kind of values does it take?

----

2. Bill makes the statement in today's RGK reading that since God is the one who makes it possible to live without impossibility, we might as well live beyond what is acceptable and normal. What are a few areas of your home and family life that you want to start applying "living beyond normal" to through this study?

----

3. God is gloriously revealed in the Gospel and is made known in many other ways. But in what way is the home one of the clearest ways that He is to be revealed?

----

4. Christ's word over the Church (washing her with it, according to Ephesians 5) brings cleansing and refreshing. Yet in many homes, people are loose with their words rather than careful. Does your conversation at home tend toward cleansing and refreshing? If not, what can you do to make that true of your words more often?

Day 4

Growing Down

Whoever then humbles himself as this child, he is the greatest in the kingdom of heaven.

Matthew 18:4

IN A CHILD'S EYES, life is an adventure. There is so much to see and enjoy and laugh about. As important as it is for our children to learn from us along the way, it is also important for us to grow down, so to speak, and learn from them. In fact, Jesus taught His disciples that they had to *become like a child*. Keeping that childlike sense of adventure in life is something we all need to learn.

That is what today's lesson is about—how our ability to lead (even as parents) is often connected to our ability to follow. Before he became ruler and king, David *followed* his father's sheep and learned a lot in the process. Great leaders know they don't know everything, and they also have a humility that is willing to follow and even to learn from those they lead.

When we receive and learn from children, it positions us to receive more of the Kingdom. As you will read in RGK today, they come together in one package.

- Today's Scripture reading: Matthew 18:18–20; Ephesians 6:1–4
- Today's reading from *Raising Giant-Killers*: the second half of chapter 2, starting at "Following Sheep"

Questions to Consider

1. In what way did Jesus exalt the role of children in the eyes of all who follow Him? Why do you think He did this?

2. Why is a humble willingness to learn from children one of our greatest opportunities for growth as parents and as people?

3. What does it mean to "receive" children? What are two notable fruits or benefits of "receiving" a child?

4. In RGK Bill tells the story of when his *No* came out wrong and he ended up square dancing with his overjoyed daughter, eight-year-old Leah. Name an experience you have had where "receiving" a child led you into enjoyment and wonder.

Session 1 Video Takeaways

- The fear of giants (in their Promised Land) intimidated Israel and put them in bondage for a long time.
- As parents, our personal victories become the inheritance of our children (as David's personal victory became Israel's inheritance).
- We are raising up a generation to be victorious and shape the course of world history.
- Jesus can work with any broken situation and make it effective.
- Two are better than one if united, but two are less than one if divided.
- It's vital that we learn how to see potential and possibilities.
- We don't want to deny the existence of a problem, but we also don't want to allow the problem a place of influence.
- Giving yourself to your children has an impact on future battles that you will face.
- We are known for what we see and believe about our family and purpose.
- There is an inward confidence embedded in the heart of a person who truly gave themselves for the sake of their children.
- One of the most important things you can teach your children (and model) is to complete a task.
- It is unusual that David followed the sheep. Shepherds are known for leading sheep.
- When we learn to pay attention to our children, we are in a sense following them.
- There are times when your idea for the day isn't as important as your children's need of the day.
- Parents who are unwilling to learn from their children are missing their greatest opportunity for growth.
- David models for us what it's like to be a parent and leader. You have to follow sheep if you are going to learn to lead sheep.

Some Cornerstones of Parenting

Frequently throughout Scripture, we see God making it possible for something to be obtained by one generation and also imparted to the next so there is never a decline in the intent and purpose of the people of God on earth. He only goes from glory to glory and has positioned us to do the same. . . .

You teach your children *when you sit, walk, lie down and rise up.* In other words, the time to teach is when you are experiencing life together. Instead of only creating a slot of teaching time, make life itself a lesson. A word of warning—preachy-type instruction gets old fast. But when we embrace the adventure called life and we discover it together, every occasion is the perfect occasion for learning insight and skills.

Raising Giant-Killers, chapter 3

Day 1

From Generation to Generation

You shall teach them [God's commands] diligently to your sons and shall talk of them when you sit in your house and when you walk by the way and when you lie down and when you rise up.

Deuteronomy 6:7

GOD MAKES IT POSSIBLE for the people of one generation to impart what they learn to the next. In fact, Deuteronomy makes it clear that it is parents who have the primary responsibility of teaching their children about the Lord and His ways. While other institutions such as the government or the school system can help teach our children certain things, it is up to us as parents to pass on the Kingdom-oriented values that help bring about "on earth as it is in heaven" from generation to generation.

How do we accomplish this? In this session we take a look at some of the ways, among them *the importance of the testimony*. I am not sure I can overstate this one or emphasize it strongly enough. *Testimonies prophesy*. When our children hear us tell a story of what God has done for us or for someone we know, it becomes a story of what He will do for them. Rather than allowing your dinner table conversation to focus on problems, bad news or gossip, steer it toward giving testimonies of things only God can do in people's lives. That is the kind of food you can grow giant-killers on!

- Today's Scripture reading: Deuteronomy 6; Psalm 78:1–8
- Today's reading from *Raising Giant-Killers*: the first half of chapter 3, through the "Testimonies Prophesy" section

Questions to Consider

1. Write down a few ways you can think of in which you can safe-guard your role as the primary influencer of your children, while also making appropriate use of the help outside institutions offer. (The "right answer" is not in the book; this is personal.)

_____

_____

_____

_____

2. Are you in the habit of teaching your children "when you sit, walk, lie down and rise up," or in other words, when you experience life together? Or do you tend to preach at your children instead? Why does teaching them work better than preaching at them?

_____

_____

_____

_____

3. Why is it important for you to share your personal God-story with your family members?

_____

_____

_____

_____

4. In what way do testimonies prophesy? What effect does that have on our young giant-killers?

_____

_____

_____

_____

Day 2

Setting the Stage

For he who comes to God must believe that He is and that He
is a rewarder of those who seek Him.

Hebrews 11:6

SINCE OUR HEAVENLY FATHER is a rewarder of those who seek Him,
one of the ways we can represent Him well to our children is by
also being rewarders of what they do that is good and right. I used
reward frequently and unapologetically with my children, and I use it
with my grandchildren, too, as you will see in today's RGK reading. We
are all built for reward, and it works!

Something else you will see in today's reading is what I call the four
cornerstones of thought—four things that can shape culture and set the
parameters for our thoughts, values, beliefs and actions. These cornerstones are vitally important for our children to recognize and adopt for
themselves. They are so important that we have even built a declaration
around them that we use in our church's children's ministry. (You can
read that at the back of RGK as appendix 3.) These cornerstones also
figure prominently in the letter I wrote my son Eric, called "10 Things
I Wanted My Children to Know" before they left home (which you can
read in RGK as appendix 1).

Using reward and passing on important cornerstones like you will
read about today are a couple of ways that we can set the stage for the
next generation's increase and blessing.

- Today's Scripture reading: Hebrews 11:1–21
- Today's reading from *Raising Giant-Killers*: the second half of chapter 3, starting at "Rewards"

Questions to Consider

1. What are some of the rewards you use in your home to give attention to what is right and to celebrate it? If you have not used reward very much with your children, what are some ways you can think of to start implementing it more effectively?

2. You read in RGK today the quote from John Adams about generational responsibility. In what way does it express the heart of God for us to live for a generation we will never see?

3. Sometimes adults are as much in need of adopting these four cornerstones as children are: 1. God is good. 2. Nothing is impossible. 3. Everything was settled at the cross. 4. I am important. What does it do in you when you make the declaration in appendix 3 about them out loud? Do you need to settle these four things in your heart first so you can then teach them to your children?

4. Bill states in RGK that if we believe God can use children, we must make room for their involvement in our efforts to love and minister to people. In what ways can you give your children more occasions to practice what they have learned about loving and serving others?

Day 3

Godly Government

I will make you exceedingly fruitful, and I will make nations
of you, and kings will come forth from you.

Genesis 17:6

PARENTS ARE governmental representatives of God. Does that sound strange at first? In today's RGK reading, you will discover how true it is. Government is a human institution created by God, to represent God. Parents are His representatives to their families, and have been set in place by Him both to protect and to empower the ones who are under their rule.

Believers (and parents) who resist the idea of ruling usually have seen others misuse or abuse their authority, and have often felt the fallout of that misuse and abuse. Yet when authority is used correctly, it represents God well. Jesus was the ultimate example of that kind of leadership.

Here is the key to implementing godly government at home (or anywhere else): *Rule with the heart of a servant, and serve with the heart of a king.*

- Today's Scripture reading: Genesis 17:1–9
- Today's reading from *Raising Giant-Killers*: the first half of chapter 4, through "Kings Were God's Idea"

Questions to Consider

1. As Bill says in RGK, whenever a person has a responsibility to govern, he or she has an obligation to find out how that authority is to be expressed. In what way is that particularly applicable to parenting? How is this study helping you accomplish that so far?

2. Why do you think it is that the two basic purposes of government, *to protect and to empower*, are best accomplished by people who know when and how to rule, and when and how to serve?

3. What does *ruling with the heart of a servant* mean to you in regard to parenting?

4. What does *serving with the heart of a king* mean to you in regard to parenting?

Day 4

To Protect and Empower

Submit yourselves for the Lord's sake to every human institution, whether to a king as the one in authority, or to governors as sent by him for the punishment of evildoers and the praise of those who do right.

1 Peter 2:13–14

WE ARE NOT ONLY PARENTS and grandparents; we are architects and builders. It takes leaders who will *protect* and *empower* to build up the next generation, and in today's lesson we take a closer look at those two concepts that are inherent in those who govern well. That includes us as parents. Nehemiah gives us a great picture of someone who builds and governs well, as you will see in today's RGK reading. He knew how to protect and empower those under his authority, even in the midst of conflict.

Protecting those under our authority requires a balance between justice and mercy. While showing mercy is personally liberating and protects us from bitterness, it is justice that encourages and rewards good over evil in society and causes fear of wrongdoing. In government, the leaders who carry out justice are called *ministers of God*.

Empowering those under our authority requires praising and encouraging the ones who are doing right. Praise fuels the hearts of those doing their best to become builders themselves, and that includes our children as they grow up into courageous giant-killers who will shape the world they live in.

- Today's Scripture reading: Romans 13:1–7; 1 Peter 2:13–17
- Today's reading from *Raising Giant-Killers*: the second half of chapter 4, starting at "Protect and Empower"

Questions to Consider

1. When you protect your children, they flourish. When you empower your children, they flourish. How do you see this mirroring what God your heavenly Father does for you as His son or daughter?

2. What is the difference between applying justice and mercy in our personal lives and applying them in a governmental role, particularly civil government?

3. Just as Nehemiah faced opposition in accomplishing his task of rebuilding the walls of Jerusalem, we face opposition in our task of parenting our children. What kind of weapons do you carry in one hand as you parent with the other, so to speak?

4. Where does your courage come from as you prayerfully protect the lives of the ones you are building up and empowering in your home?

Session 2 Video Takeaways

- All government (whether in the home, a corporation, or a nation) has two basic functions:

  1. To protect

  2. To empower

- Your first responsibility is for yourself, your children and your household. (Don't be manipulated by false mercy.)

- Much of Kingdom culture was actually established in Israel's culture as a nation.

- We either become intentional in how we train and raise our children, or our lack of intentionality (our lack of decision making) leaves room for them to be taught by other voices.

- God gave the responsibility to teach children to parents, not to government.

- Teachers and school systems are delegated authority appointed by you.

- Take your high points and points of breakthrough in God, and make them known to your children. (Make sure they know your history in God.)

- An inheritance is when we receive something for free that someone else paid a price for.

- If you're going to leave an inheritance to your children, you will need to pay a price to increase what you got for free.

- Prophecy has two basic functions:

  1. Foretells the future

  2. Changes the present

- The testimony of Jesus is the spirit of prophecy (Revelation 19:10).

- Anytime we report on what God has done, we are prophesying not only what He is going to do, but in some cases we are changing the present context in which God is going to work in that person's life.

- Every context in life has a place to unfold life (i.e., this is what it looks like . . .).

- Always have the stories of the impossible bowing before the name of Jesus.

- We get to tell our kids what God is like, and we get to do it through stories.

Parents as Builders

It is a great bonus to see children grow up in our homes to represent an aspect of God's nature in an honest and wholesome way. This helps create legacy. And legacy cannot be overrated. King David left a mark on God's heart that was so significant that several hundred years later, God treated people with an increased measure of favor because they were David's descendants. That is remarkable. Touching the heart of God with our faithfulness and creating a legacy that favors multiple generations should be the goal of every believing household.

Raising Giant-Killers, chapter 5

Day 1

Building Materials

We love, because He first loved us.

1 John 4:19

I F WE ARE GOING TO BE architects and designers of families, individuals and legacies, as chapter 5 in the RGK book suggests, it is our job to come up with a plan for what we are building. Then we need to be intentional about making our plan come to life, and part of that is deciding what materials—what building blocks—best suit our design. Today and in Day 2 just ahead, we will look at the building blocks I consider the most essential for carrying out our parenting plan successfully.

It almost goes without saying that the greatest building block of a healthy home and family is *love*. We model the way we love our families on the greatest example of love the world has ever known—the sacrificial love of Jesus on the cross. God's love is perfect love, and as I say in RGK today, living with love, the cornerstone of behavior, sets the boundaries for life.

Other things we will look at today are *peace* (expressed in the atmosphere of a home), *principles* (the values of the Kingdom) and *endurance* (working through pain, toward eternal gain). Each of these is another essential building block of home and family.

- Today's Scripture reading: 1 John 4:7–21
- Today's reading from *Raising Giant-Killers*: the first half of chapter 5, through "Endurance"

Questions to Consider

1. Why is it so important that the husband/father be responsible to set the standard of love in the home and love sacrificially?

2. In what way is the atmosphere of peace that the wife is responsible to set in the home "presence-based"?

3. Think about a time when it felt as if God left you alone to test you and see what was in your heart, as He did with Hezekiah. What did you learn about yourself in that time? Why are such moments vital in seeing how much of His glory we can carry?

4. Trying to be consistent as a parent can be painful, when the alternative—compromising to lessen the discomfort of a moment—would be so much easier. What example of this challenge can you think of in your parenting? Why is it worth enduring the pain rather than taking the easy way out?

Day 2

Model Parents

Let your light shine before men in such a way that they may
see your good works, and glorify your Father who is in heaven.

Matthew 5:16

TODAY, WE LOOK at another three essential building blocks of a
healthy home: *hope*, *character* and *purpose*. Hope is the heartbeat
of heaven and has to be the heartbeat of a home. If there is any
area about our home and family in which we feel hopeless, something
is the matter! Hopelessness is a red flag telling us that something is
undermining our family's health and well-being, and that we need to
address it.

While character is important to instill in our children, when I talk
about it as a building block, I mean *our* character as parents and people.
The character traits we live out in front of our children help build character in them, because everything we teach our kids has greater authority
when we model it first in our own lives. In RGK today, I talk about some
character traits every parent should aim to model for his or her children.

Finally, living with purpose is vital. This world needs to see Jesus
in and through His people, and part of our design is to be His eternal
dwelling place, His house. We represent Him—or as I like to say, we
re-present Him—in how we live and love. Young giant-killers who learn
this have great effect on the world around them.

- Today's Scripture reading: Matthew 5:13–16; Romans 5:1–5
- Today's reading from *Raising Giant-Killers*: the second half of chapter 5, starting at "Hope"

Questions to Consider

1. When we feel hopeless as parents (or in any area of life), what have we stepped out of, and what have we forgotten? What must we do until hope is restored?

_____

_____

_____

_____

2. If you require something of your child, why must it be found in your life first?

_____

_____

_____

_____

3. Look again at the important areas Bill mentioned in RGK today that we must model for our children (under the "Character" heading). Which one or two do you already model well? Which one or two do you need the most practice in? What steps will you take to become an even better model in those areas?

_____

_____

_____

_____

4. What do you think it does to young giant-killers when they discover that they were designed to be the dwelling place of God? What does it do to people looking on, who see our children's representation or revelation of Him?

_____

_____

_____

_____

Day 3

React or Respond?

Speaking the truth in love, we are to grow up in all aspects into Him who is the head, even Christ.

Ephesians 4:15

GIVING A THOUGHTFUL RESPONSE to something is miles ahead of having a knee-jerk reaction. Yet many parents often react to things that arise in the course of their parenting, when there is a much better course of action. As you will see in today's lesson, it is better to become a first responder, not a first reactor. It is what Jesus did. Rather than reacting to the devil, He spent His time responding to the Father. We need to adopt His attitude in order to parent effectively, with intention and purpose.

Communication is key in responding, not reacting. In today's reading I talk about what I call the communications war, along with a number of strategies that will help you win that war as intentional parents. The powers of darkness work hard to divide people in this area, but we can succeed in communicating well with each other inside and outside the family, and we can teach our children to do the same.

- Today's Scripture reading: Proverbs 27:10; Ephesians 4:11–16
- Today's reading from *Raising Giant-Killers*: the first half of chapter 6, through "Our Home—Safe and Fun"

Questions to Consider

1. Think about the kind of reentry scenario that typically happens in your home. How do you tend to react to each other coming in the door? Do you bring up conflict or difficulties right away, or do you respond to each other with warm, positive greetings that make everyone want to regroup? If you have not done so already, agree together (as Bill and Beni did early on) never to greet each other negatively.

2. To win the communications war, it is important to stay away from assuming that you know another person's motives. Why is it important to help your children develop that particular ability?

3. What do you do when one of your children interrupts a conversation you are having with another adult? What would you think of responding the way Bill talked about instead in the "Interruptions with Purpose" section of today's RGK reading?

4. Beni drew the Johnson kids and their friends into deep conversation time and again by allowing them to open up about anything without shocking her, and by treating them with honor, respect and total honesty. Are there those in your children's circle of friends who could use a safe and caring adult to talk life over with? What can you do to become that person for them?

Day 4

Attitudes of the Heart

Watch over your heart with all diligence, for from it flow the springs of life.

Proverbs 4:23

YOU WILL READ THIS in the pages of the book today, but it is worth reading twice: *Attitude is paramount. Academics are important, but the heart is more important.*

If you focus on correcting attitude first with your kids, it can prevent having to deal with bad conduct later. That is why you will read today about how I always checked attitude first on my kids' report cards. And after their attitude marks, I looked at their grade in Bible (they attended a Christian school). To be successful, they needed a foundation in the Word of God (which you must provide for your kids if their school does not). After attitude and Bible marks, I then looked at their academic grades. But the academics always fell in line anyway, as long as our kids were doing well in their heart attitudes and devotion to God's Word.

That is how it worked for us, and no doubt you will find it the same for your family. It is all about the heart. Academics can be studied and skill can be taught, and both are important. But any lasting success starts with having the right heart.

- Today's Scripture reading: Matthew 8:5–13; Luke 7:1–10; Acts 13:22
- Today's reading from *Raising Giant-Killers*: the second half of chapter 6, starting at "Expectations Rule"

Questions to Consider

1. What kinds of expectations about attitude rule your house? How are you teaching your kids that when they slay the giants on the inside (for example, bad attitudes), they will then find success on the outside?

_____

_____

_____

_____

2. Have you taken the approach with your children (and grandchildren) that skills can be learned, but that heart is greater than skills? What are some ways you can reinforce this in your parenting?

_____

_____

_____

_____

3. In the "Delegated Authority" section of the book, Bill states that to do core values well, there must be an understanding of Kingdom authority. How do your children do at respecting delegated authority? What adjustments need to be made in this area?

_____

_____

_____

_____

4. In what ways do you model Kingdom authority for your children? What are some ways you can help them understand authority better from God's perspective?

_____

_____

_____

_____

Session 3 Video Takeaways

- A father is responsible for the standard of love in the home. A mother is responsible for the atmosphere.
- The husband sets the level of sacrifice, which is love.
- Atmosphere is a presence-based culture. Heaven itself is a presence-based culture.
- Never greet your spouse with conflict or difficulty unless it is an emergency.
- One of the most important things both husband and wife contribute to an atmosphere is the issue of hope.
- We have the reason to be the most hope-filled people on the planet.
- There are always more reasons to hope than there are not to, especially when you get into God's Word and see what He is saying.
- Jesus didn't react to the devil; He responded to what the Father was doing.
- As parents, we learn to respond instead of react.
- You want to build in everybody in your household an instinctive desire to be home.
- Good communication happens when people don't feel threatened for sharing their opinion.
- Ask your children to share when they have a success in life, so that they can be in contact with what they are feeling.
- Paupers talk about people; kings talk about ideas and potential.
- When the other person feels valued, they will always be more inclined to say what they are thinking.
- Always specifically say what you are sorry for, and then have the person doing the forgiving specifically mention what they forgive.
- Never assume you know the motive of another person.
- God opens up something to give us insight for prayer, but never for attack.
- If you can correct attitude, you can prevent bad conduct.
- Don't allow children to say, "It's not fair."
- I can't control what I start with, but I do have influence over where I end.
- Faithfulness in small things brings increase.
- If I'm faithful with what God's given me, He will increase my sphere of influence.

Discipline and Reward

It is important to realize that it is never too late to start parenting intentionally. If your kids are older (preteen and up) and you have not been an intentional parent, sit down and have an open conversation with them. Tell them, "I've not done what I should as a parent. I didn't know it, and now I'm trying to make changes because I believe in you kids, and I want you to succeed in life." And talk about setting new and necessary boundaries. Kids of any age have a built-in need for boundaries; they want to explore in safety. Try to come to some understanding of what works well for your kids at their current ages. Start with honor, and with reward for doing what is right, but make clear the consequences for doing what is wrong. Stack the deck with positive things, but set consequences for wrong decisions as well. And then respond to your children, rather than reacting emotionally as your default parenting method. It will change the atmosphere of your entire household.

Raising Giant-Killers, chapter 7

Day 1

The Process for Discipline

He disciplines us for our good, so that we may share His holiness.

Hebrews 12:10

Just as God disciplines us for our good, we discipline our children for their good. At least, that should be the case. It is important for us to check our motives and be sure, because disciplining our children is never meant to be for us. Some parents get in the habit of using discipline as a means of releasing their frustration or anger, but that does more harm than good and can lead to abuse. As I tell you in this session's video, I never approached an occasion of discipline when I was angry. I would send my child to his or her room first, and then I would wait to follow until I was ready to carry out discipline for the *child's* benefit.

I do believe in spanking, and in today's RGK reading I talk more about that. But any discipline, including spanking, ought to be a process—an event in which we take the time to do it appropriately and for the right reasons. That is the kind of discipline that will bring the right result. In fact, if discipline is done well, it endears us to people, not drives us apart. As you will read, my children would often come sit on my lap after being disciplined, because even the way I carried it out reassured them that I loved them.

- Today's Scripture reading: Hebrews 12:4–14
- Today's reading from *Raising Giant-Killers*: the first half of chapter 7, through "My Personal Process for Discipline"

Questions to Consider

1. Based on Hebrews 12:7–8, in what ways does discipline prove that you belong? Based on that, what does appropriate discipline, carried out appropriately, say to a child's heart?

2. What is the difference between discipline as an outburst and discipline as an occasion? Evaluate which of these is the more consistent pattern in your home. What do you need to change to do better in this area?

3. What happens when instead of following a child's disobedience, discipline follows a parent's anger? If that has been your pattern of discipline, what will you do to recalibrate your children—and yourself?

4. Real discipline takes time. Are you taking the necessary time to carry it out well? In RGK, Bill wrote about his personal process for discipline. What parts of his procedure might help you if you apply them in your home?

Day 2

Proverbs on Discipline

Correct your son, and he will give you comfort; he will also delight your soul.

Proverbs 29:17

THE BOOK OF PROVERBS is full of insights on discipline that are just too good to miss. The ones you will read about today in RGK reinforce the things we talked about in Day 1, and they show the tenderness and concern that are so necessary for us to have as we parent with divine purpose to achieve eternal results.

We must have the same tender heart toward our children that Paul expressed toward the believers in Thessalonica, which you will also read about. He used the language of home and family—words like *tender care* and *fond affection*—to reveal his heart for the Church. Intentional parenting is all about words like that. Such words are not the opposite of discipline; they embody it. The heart we put into discipline now will train our children not only to become giant-killers, but also to become future intentional parents themselves.

- Today's Scripture reading: Ephesians 5:1–21
- Today's reading from *Raising Giant-Killers*: the second half of chapter 7, starting at "My Repentance"

Questions to Consider

1. Have you ever had to repent to your family, as Bill did in the first story he told in RGK today? Even if you sometimes fail to lead by example in doing right, what does it say to your kids if you at least lead by example in repentance afterward?

2. If we ignore discipline now because of inconvenience or the wisdom of the day, our children will pay the price later. What kinds of things does discipline now rescue our children from later?

3. Bill's friend Shawn Bolz says that God allows our closest friends to see our idiosyncrasies so they will always know that when God uses us, it is always by grace. How does that apply in the context of parenting and what your children see in you?

4. As a parent, you undoubtedly recognize that each of your children is unique. In what ways has the wisdom of God helped you recognize that the process you use for disciplining one child might need to be different for another?

Day 3

Bribery or Reward?

Let us consider how to stimulate one another to love and good deeds.

Hebrews 10:24

IN SESSION 2 we talked about how God is a rewarder of those who seek Him. Modeling our parenting after our heavenly Father, Beni and I also used rewards. When our young children sought God by participating in worship during church services, we bought them ice cream afterward. Unashamedly.

Some would call that *bribery*. We called it *reward*. Today and in Day 4, we will be talking about how to train our children to know God. We did whatever it took to stimulate our kids to love and good deeds, and we did whatever it took to turn their attention to their heavenly Father.

Today in RGK and in Scripture, you will read about how the boy Samuel was trained from an early age to serve in the house of the Lord, and about how young Solomon was trained to seek after God's wisdom and help. We have the same goals as intentional parents. Our training along these lines sets up a momentum that attracts the voice of God into our kids' lives at an early age. And once they have their own personal encounter with God, it won't even take ice cream rewards anymore. He becomes reward enough.

- Today's Scripture reading: Luke 1:39–45; 1 Samuel 3:1–10
- Today's reading from *Raising Giant-Killers*: the first half of chapter 8, through "Raising Royalty"

Questions to Consider

1. Has attending church been nonnegotiable in your household? What have you seen your young children pick up spiritually as a result? If church has been negotiable, what is your new family plan after going through this lesson?

_____

_____

_____

_____

2. Why is bringing our children into a holy atmosphere and exposing them to the glory of God one of the best gifts we can give them?

_____

_____

_____

_____

3. What did reading about the boy Samuel's training show you about training children to do something simply because it is right spiritually, even before they completely understand it?

_____

_____

_____

_____

4. What did reading about young Solomon's instruction from his father, David, show you about how aggressively instructing our children carries prophetic significance?

_____

_____

_____

_____

Day 4

Faithfulness Rewarded

For to everyone who has, more shall be given, and he will have
an abundance.

Matthew 25:29

THINK ABOUT WHAT YOU DO in work and ministry. Do your kids
pay a price for who you are, as my kids did with me? That is often
the case, yet as parents we can offset some of that cost through
reward. We can look for opportunities to bless our kids because of our
position. While "nepotism" is politically incorrect, reward is spiritually
savvy.

Again, reward is a biblical concept, and God Himself is a rewarder.
You will read today in RGK about how David sought reward, and about
how Jesus' parable about the talents demonstrated that reward is given
to the faithful. We don't all have the same abilities, but in the Kingdom
we all have the chance to succeed, and we all have the chance for reward.

It is important that we teach our children these concepts about faithfulness and reward. As I tell you in the book, in the Kingdom there is
no lid on the potential of someone who learns to be faithful and bring
increase for the King.

- Today's Scripture reading: 1 Samuel 17:20–30; Matthew 25:14–30
- Today's reading from *Raising Giant-Killers*: the second half of chapter 8, starting at "Cost and Reward"

Questions to Consider

1. What price do your kids pay for the work/ministry you are involved in? What rewards can you make available to them as a result, simply for being your children?

_____

_____

_____

_____

2. When David sought reward, his oldest brother accused him out of fear and maybe even jealousy. Jealousy toward those who are blessed is at an all-time high these days, but what happens when people label jealousy as a virtue under other names?

_____

_____

_____

_____

3. Bill told you in today's reading how he and Beni would respond if their children tried to say, "That's not fair!" Have your children raised that cry of protest with you? How will your answer to them change in response to today's lesson?

_____

_____

_____

_____

4. What is the difference in effectiveness between celebrating the efforts of our children for trying something, and giving them trophies for doing nothing but showing up?

_____

_____

_____

_____

Session 4 Video Takeaways

- Every institution's strength is in its ability to discipline.
- Discipline helps children to learn that there are consequences for choices.
- The problem in many homes is that discipline is for the sake of the parent, not the child.
- To discipline correctly takes time.
- Make discipline an event.
- Never scold or embarrass children in front of friends. Always work to protect their dignity.
- We never used our hands for discipline. Hands are for affection, touch, love and compassion.
- If discipline is done well, it endears us to people, not drives us from them.
- Discipline helps to refine focus, refine purpose and understanding of destiny.
- We train our children to respond to what we say (not our volume).
- It takes a child seven positive comments to recover from one negative comment.
- From a very early age, we would "pull out the gold" in our children.
- It's important to posture yourself to see what's good, what's right.
- A part of our understanding of faith is that God is a rewarder.
- Reward has to be built into our relationships, specifically starting at home.
- Whatever you give attention to will increase.

Hearing from God as Parents

We have the privilege and responsibility to pray over our children. Praying prayers that the Holy Spirit says *amen* to is one of the greatest joys ever. In doing so, we become involved in bringing the heart, as well as the hand, of God to our families. Learning to recognize the Holy Spirit's response to what you pray helps bring exponential increase to the effectiveness of your prayers. . . .

If you will keep prayer a two-way conversation, you will discover the beauty of prayers inspired by the Holy Spirit. By learning to recognize Him in your prayers, you will be entrusted with the honor of revealing His heart at a whole new level. Whenever we discover that great treasure, we see where we can co-labor with the Lord to see His purposes in our family line. This kind of praying takes time, insight and persistence. He is moved by this in a profound way and adds the weightiness of His presence to it all.

Raising Giant-Killers, chapter 10

Day 1

God Still Speaks

Pursue love, yet desire earnestly spiritual gifts, but especially that you may prophesy.

1 Corinthians 14:1

WHILE NOTHING replaces the standard of Scripture, it is nonetheless true that God still speaks. He will talk to us as parents about a specific child or a need in our home, and if we will listen, His insight and direction will make all the difference between mere survival and living an abundant life.

I realize that most average parents simply don't see themselves as prophets, but it is not a matter of having a prophetic gift. The "office" or position of parenting itself comes with some gifts of God—among them the ability to gain a prophetic sense of what God is doing in your children's lives over the years. The more you pray *Spirit-led prayers* for your household, with a sense of surrender to God's will, not your own, the more you will pick up on God's heart for your children and their future. Anointed prayers are very similar to prophecies.

As you go through the lessons in this session about how prayer and the prophetic relate to parenting, ask God to give you greater insight and prophetic perspective about your children's place in the world and His divine purposes for them. Your goal and His are the same: for you to raise giant-killers who know His heart and show it to the world.

- Today's Scripture reading: Luke 1:67–79
- Today's reading from *Raising Giant-Killers*: the first half of chapter 9, through "Prophetic Friends"

Questions to Consider

1. As a parent seeking prophetic direction, what safeguards can you put in place to make sure you are building on the Rock, Jesus Christ, and the Word of God, rather than on subjective opinion (that could be in conflict with the Word)?

2. Bill tells you in today's RGK reading about the file Bethel Church keeps on each child in its church programs, which includes any prophetic words about that child. Why do you think it is so important to keep reinforcing to our children *what God says about them*?

3. We already talked about how we are all born into a war. One of the major battles for every person is the fight for identity. How will you use the prophetic perspective you gain as a parent to help your children win that fight?

4. What happens when parents pray their own will for their children? What happens when parents pray *Spirit-led prayers* for them?

Day 2

En-Courage Your Children

Train up a child *in the way he [or she] should go*, even when
he is old he will not depart from it.

Proverbs 22:6, emphasis added

IT IS OUR PRIVILEGE as parents to exercise the faith factor and expect
the Lord to move on behalf of our children. Yet at the same time, we
have to watch our other expectations. Trouble will result if we expect
our children to make our own disappointed dreams come true, or even
if we expect them to realize the same dreams that we were successful
in bringing to life. Each child is unique, with a uniquely divine purpose
and God-given dreams of his or her own. That is why it is so vital to
train children up in the way they should go.

I tell you the story in RGK today about my son Brian's abrupt switch
from sports to music in high school. If ever parents faced a challenge in
letting a child follow his dreams, that time in Brian's life was it for us!
In retrospect, deciding to encourage our son in his musical pursuits was
one of the best decisions Beni and I ever made as parents.

Encouragement pays off. As I say in RGK, encouragement is one of
the primary ways we empower people to become all God intended. And
that is our role as parents—to instill in our young giant-killers the courage to become all God intends.

- Today's Scripture reading: John 5:12; 12:49; Mark 7:24–30
- Today's reading from *Raising Giant-Killers*: the second half of chapter 9, starting at "Jesus' Personal Key"

Questions to Consider

1. The Syrophoenician woman who asked Jesus to heal her daughter exercised the faith factor in the face of difficulty. What issue is your household facing right now that you need to respond to by exercising the faith factor? In what way are you expecting that the Lord will move on behalf of your child (or children)?

_____

_____

_____

_____

_____

2. Did your parents encourage you to pursue your dreams, or did they encourage you to pursue their dreams for you? How did their expectations affect you? What are some things you learned from that time in your life that you can put to use in parenting your children?

_____

_____

_____

_____

_____

3. Think back on the last 24 hours and compare the number of positive comments versus the number of corrective comments you made to your children. Are you anywhere near the 7:1 ratio that is necessary if the positive comments are going to offset the corrections? If not, what will you do to become a better encourager?

_____

_____

_____

_____

_____

4. Why do you think it is true that we are more likely to recognize the hand of God on a life when we are invested in that person's well-being through prayer?

_____

_____

_____

_____

_____

_____

Day 3

The Timing of Job

Job would send and consecrate them, rising up early in the morning and offering burnt offerings according to the number of them all.

Job 1:5

As you will see in today's lesson, Job really knew how to cover his children in prayer. There is a lesson for us in his timing, and in his commitment to praying for his children. Like Job, we are the watchmen over our houses (whether as a father or a mother). We watch for the challenges our families face, we seek God's promises for victory and we cover our kids in prayer.

Beni and I consistently prayed for our children at night before bed. Certainly it was about having some powerful supernatural moments in prayer over them, but it was also about the discipline of consistency. We took the time to work the yeast of our prayers into the dough of their lives, with the goal of helping them rise to their potential. We "called out the gold" in our kids, mixing God's promises with our confessions and decrees. Do the same for your children and watch them rise.

- Today's Scripture reading: Isaiah 9:2–7
- Today's reading from *Raising Giant-Killers*: the first half of chapter 10, through "Good Words, Bad Words"

Questions to Consider

1. In what ways are anointed prayers very similar to authentic prophetic words?

   _____

   _____

   _____

   _____

2. It is important to learn to recognize prayers that attract the Holy Spirit. In today's RGK pages, Bill wrote about some of the ways he recognizes the Holy Spirit's response to his prayers. What are some of the ways you recognize His response? What does that do to the effectiveness of your prayers?

   _____

   _____

   _____

   _____

3. Bill often used to tell his kids to ask God if there was anything impossible He wanted them to do, and that they were part of a team that was here to change the world. What kinds of things do you tell your children that will challenge their faith and shape their thought life (without pressuring them to perform)?

   _____

   _____

   _____

   _____

4. Are you good at flushing the bad words careless people speak about your children, as Bill and Beni were, or are you more likely to entertain people's "sense of humor" and "just wait" stories? What are the benefits of flushing those kinds of words immediately?

   _____

   _____

   _____

   _____

Day 4

Seeding the Clouds of Destiny

I will give them a heart to know Me, for I am the Lord.
                                                    Jeremiah 24:7

WE SEED THE CLOUDS of destiny over our families every day with what we do and what we say. Speaking the promises of God from Scripture over our children is therefore one of the most powerful things we can do in raising them to be giant-killers.

My mother knew this well. She had a whole list of Scriptures she would pray over her children and their children, and now even their children. She passed her list on to me and to all the parents in our family, and now I am passing that list on to you as appendix 4 in the book. Let this list become one of your most valuable tools for intentional parenting. As an intentional parent, you will then become the tool in God's hands that He uses to shape the character and destiny of your children's lives.

- Today's Scripture reading: Isaiah 54:13–17
- Today's reading from *Raising Giant-Killers*: the second half of chapter 10, starting at "Don't Be Ignorant"

Questions to Consider

1. From two-year-olds to teens, every childhood age has its detractors. Write down some positive responses you can have ready the next time you talk with a detractor who is being negative about childhood. Think about the response of Bill's uncle to the terrible twos as an example: "Every household needs a two-year-old in it" (just to keep us from materialism).

   _____

   _____

   _____

   _____

   _____

2. Think about experiences you may have had with your kids that were similar to Bill's when Eric came and told him he hated English class. Why does it help our children to see a purpose for their pain or difficulty? In what way do divine perspectives always bring hope?

   _____

   _____

   _____

   _____

   _____

3. Bill tells you in RGK how excited he became when he realized that his prayer for his kids to have a heart to know God was an echo of Jeremiah 24:7. What prayers have you prayed over your children that you later discovered were biblical prayers? (If you don't have any biblical prayers for them yet, turn to appendix 4 in the book and adopt some from Bill's mother's list.)

   _____

   _____

   _____

   _____

4. Why is it vital not only that we learn to pray the promises of God from Scripture as intentional parents, but that we also teach our children to use this tool themselves?

_____

_____

_____

_____

_____

_____

Session 5 Video Guide

- Anointed prayers are very similar to prophecies.
- Pray for your children not because you anticipate them doing wrong, but to help them and build courage in them.
- Pray over each child uniquely according to the gift that is inside each one.
- Give your children a purpose for difficulty.
- You see, and you speak. You see, and you declare.
- Your family has a specific call on their lives, but it doesn't predetermine their occupation.
- Refuse to entertain bad words over your children.
- Make a decision that you are going to enjoy every single age that your children enter into.
- Your children need to know they were born to do impossible things.
- Your children need to know they are here as part of the team that is to change the world.
- Feed into the gift and calling that God has put on your children.
- Brag on your children in front of other adults and their peers.
- Take time to build up the creative expression that is inside your children.
- Notice detail about what your children notice detail about.
- Find Scriptures for your family, and pray them until they become yours.
- Hear from God over different family members. Hold those things before the Lord.
- If I have an idea that is different than God's idea, then mine dies and His is embraced.
- If I have an idea that is the same as His, then I know where I got it.

Government for Giant-Killers

We are raising our children to change the world. Literally. To bring change well, they will need to understand culture, government, justice and education. It is vital for them to perceive the nature of biblical culture, which is the opposite of the politically correct mantra of the day. The politically correct approach is without Christ and sounds like wisdom, although it is the gibberish of fools. It is not that we need to become like another Israel. But it is vital for us to see how God says a society should function. Godly government is distinct in that by nature, it provides protection and empowerment. These things must become central to our children's ambition and strategy for how to bring change.

Raising Giant-Killers, chapter 11

Day 1

Government at Home

For the weapons of our warfare are not of the flesh, but divinely powerful for the destruction of fortresses.

2 Corinthians 10:4

GOVERNMENT HAS ITS PLACE in society. Even big government has its place. But the place government does not have is parenting children. It cannot and should not occupy your place as a parent. It is your God-given privilege to be the party responsible for raising your children. God designed parents to carry authority over their families, and there is no substitute in your children's lives for *you*.

There are some fill-ins who can help you along the way, of course. For example, dedicated teachers in the educational system can be of great value in teaching your children specific skills like reading and math. We will talk a lot in today's lesson about how to work with such professionals and not against them, to the benefit of everyone.

It is true that in our culture, we live in the midst of a bombardment of demonic ideals coming from every direction. And it is true that we have a primary responsibility to raise our children with passion and devotion to the truth. Yet it is also true that we can accomplish that goal in the context of love. We will talk a lot about that, too.

- Today's Scripture reading: Philippians 4:4–9
- Today's reading from *Raising Giant-Killers*: the first half of chapter 11, through "The Problem with Truth"

Questions to Consider

1. The good intentions of government cannot replace the wisdom of God's design for the family. Are you facing challenges in your part of the world over the problem of *who gets to raise a child*? How do you respond with both truth and love?

2. Do you believe that the answer to fixing most of the ills of society is healthy family life? How might that be so?

3. If your children are involved with the public school system, in what ways have you shown love through having a servant's heart, with the ultimate goal of affecting that educational environment? What kinds of results have you seen?

4. What does it mean to say that light (seeing truth) requires greater amounts of love if we are to remain in the center of Jesus' heart for this world?

Day 2

Big Picture Hope

O taste and see that the LORD is good.
Psalm 34:8

WE NEED TO LEARN how God says a society should function, and then teach that to our children. It is also essential that we teach our kids how biblical government operates, in contrast to what they may see modeled around them in their culture and country. Then what do we do next, since much of the world around us does not function according to God's laws or governmental design? As we talked about in Day 1, we go out and model the truth in love.

When will "on earth as it is in heaven" become more of a reality? When we have parents who *think*, raising children who *think*, who are all willing to get into the middle of this world's muck and bring change! Giant-killers live out transformation in such a way that the people who see it become hungry for the Kingdom.

That is why I spent time talking about government in a book on parenting. Not to vent or to highlight the ills of society, but to bring hope for the big picture. Because our children who understand Kingdom government bring hope for a better future.

- Today's Scripture reading: Psalm 34:1–14
- Today's reading from *Raising Giant-Killers*: the second half of chapter 11, starting at "Insanity or Compassion?"

Questions to Consider

1. What do you see as the difference between compassion and what Bill calls in the book "unsanctified mercy"? How does unsanctified mercy tip the balance between human rights and human responsibilities?

   _____

   _____

   _____

   _____

2. When it comes to controversy, what does it mean to say that the absence of opposition is not favor; it is simply a form of peace that is not Kingdom?

   _____

   _____

   _____

   _____

3. What was your response to the statement Bill made in RGK that chanting religious values and quoting Scriptures from a book people hold no value for do not bring change? What ways have you and your family found to model and proclaim the principles of God's Kingdom in ways that do bring change?

   _____

   _____

   _____

   _____

4. The lifestyle of the Kingdom of God is very attractive and *biblically* logical, if displayed correctly. What attracted you to it before you were a believer? What do you think attracts others to it when they see it displayed in you? Talk with your children about how they can display the Kingdom in ways that bring forth fruit desirable to all.

   _____

   _____

   _____

   _____

Day 3

Practical Revival

Jesus was also baptized, and while He was praying, heaven was opened, and the Holy Spirit descended upon Him in bodily form like a dove.

Luke 3:21–22

THE POWER OF OUR TRANSFORMATION at salvation was never meant to be confined only within the four walls of the Church. Likewise, the effects of revival and spiritual reformation were never meant to be confined only within the spirit realm. Today's lesson is all about how every revival contains the seeds of societal reformation—provided that the people affected by it will learn to translate the effects into practical daily living.

Change *can* come to society through great outpourings of the Holy Spirit, and demonstrating that fact to our children is important. They need to learn about and be exposed to great moves of God, and they need to know how to bring about societal reformation as a result—by going out from those kinds of experiences believing that God has answers for every issue in society, and that the answers can come through them.

Believers ought to be contributors to the well-being of their cities and nations, both in prayer and in action. One of the most practical ways you and I can accomplish that is by becoming intentional parents who will raise world-changers.

- Today's Scripture reading: Luke 3:15–22
- Today's reading from *Raising Giant-Killers*: the first half of chapter 12, through "Taking Responsibility"

Questions to Consider

1. Have you educated yourself and talked with your children about any of the great moves of God throughout recent history, particularly those that had a widespread effect on society? If not, how will you begin to do this more?

_____

_____

_____

_____

2. Were you surprised to read that in the United States, the cities with the largest churchgoing population have the worst social statistics? What does raising giant-killers have to do with helping turn the tide in the opposite direction?

_____

_____

_____

_____

3. Are you the sort of believer who tends to want people to come into the places you are comfortable with (for example, your church) before you minister to them? After today's lesson, what value and importance can you see in also going out?

_____

_____

_____

_____

4. In what ways has your local church adopted the issues that surround you in your city? List a few issues here in which you see that more could be done.

_____

_____

_____

_____

Day 4

Leaving a Spiritual Wake

And he called . . . and said unto them, Occupy till I come.

Luke 19:13 KJV

IN TODAY'S RGK PAGES, I talk about a time when one segment of America's Christian population was so focused on Jesus' return that they neglected to prepare themselves to occupy productively and serve in society until He gets here. This country still feels the effects of that scenario today. Let's not let it happen again as we raise our young giant-killers. We need this next generation of Jesus lovers to pursue their places of influence in life on the earth until He comes again.

Think of the impact Esther, Daniel and Joseph had on the cultures they lived in. As you will read in RGK, they had not only personal, but even national and international results. They did their homework and were faithful to say yes to all God called them to. Our children can do the same, learning what the power of God looks like and how to operate in it. As they gain the wisdom to serve, and as they help shape the value system of their culture and nation, they will leave a spiritual wake for generations to come.

- Today's Scripture reading: Luke 19:11–27
- Today's reading from *Raising Giant-Killers*: the second half of chapter 12, starting at "The Jesus People Movement"

Questions to Consider

1. While it is wonderful for your kids to have a sense of anticipation about Jesus' return, what are some ways you can encourage them to pursue their place of influence in life while they are waiting for that event?

2. Instead of ignoring what is going on in the world, what happens when Christians are planted in systems as loving servants? What positive examples of that can you think of to talk with your children about?

3. What are some ways that revival is translated into transformational impact?

4. God is practical, and sometimes we are not. Do you believe, as the Reformers did, that He has answers for every issue of life? How does that belief affect the way you are raising your children?

Session 6 Video Guide

- The great reformers had impact on the course of history because they believed the Bible had practical answers for every question in life.
- We need to be planted in systems as loving servants so that we can influence them.
- It's vital that we think long-term.
- Raise your children to shape education and government.
- The political and religious systems work through manipulation and control. The Kingdom works through influence.
- We are to enhance what exists. That's why the Kingdom is called leaven.
- God's ideal is that the people of God would live in peace.
- We want to be used by God to build society as God meant it to be.
- "And must we, now in Christ, with shame confess, Our Love was greater, when our Light was less?" —Charles Wesley
- "We've murdered love with truth." —Jack Taylor
- We have the privilege of loving people we do not agree with.
- We serve to enhance what God has already instilled in the lives of the people we are around.
- Government has the responsibility to protect and to empower.
- The more sin there is, the more government you need.
- Never use truth as an example to hate or reject someone, but what we must do is hold to the truth of Scripture.
- We've got to restore our cities and nations to biblical standards.
- Speak the language of the people you are with, but bring the principles of the Kingdom of God into that environment.
- Take the truth of Scripture, model it, and put it into other people's language, because truth always bears fruit.
- We need the wisdom to know how to speak the language of Scripture in the language of the people.
- The Kingdom empowers you to see what you were born for.
- We don't change the culture by revolting. We change it by planting vision in the hearts of our kids.

Sexuality
by Design

Sex was intended for pleasure, according to God's design and within the context He designed it for. Raising children to embrace God's design for our sexuality positions them for living the ultimate lifestyle of joy, pleasure and fulfillment in this area. The purpose behind biblical training is not only to keep our children away from the things that destroy, but also to enable them to enter fully into the life of pleasure that God has willed for each married person. This is sexuality done well, and it must be the goal of every parent to protect and empower his or her children in this area.

Raising Giant-Killers, chapter 13

Day 1

Trusting the Designer

It is the blessing of the Lord that makes rich, and He adds no sorrow to it.

Proverbs 10:22

IT IS A SMART MOVE to trust the Designer of all life, who created so many things with the ultimate goal of our pleasure in mind. Sex is among those things, designed by God for both our procreation and pleasure. When we approach sex as He meant us to, in the context of marriage, it enriches our lives and adds no sorrow to us.

It is when we approach our sexuality outside the context He designed it for that trouble comes our way. It is important to teach our children that God created rules and boundaries around sex not because He is against us enjoying it, but because He wants to ensure that we do.

That is what today's lesson is about: helping our children understand that sexual self-control is not just about saying *no* to the wrong things; it is about saying *yes* to the right thing—a joyful, fulfilling marriage begun in purity and power.

- Today's Scripture reading: 1 Corinthians 6:12–20
- Today's reading from *Raising Giant-Killers*: the first few pages of chapter 13, through "Purity, with a Ring to It"

Questions to Consider

1. What is the difference between having the breakthroughs of life come from the hand of God and having them come through our own hands? How does that relate to our experience of sexual pleasures?

   _____

   _____

   _____

   _____

   _____

   _____

2. In view of Kris Vallotton's statement that the first one to teach on a subject creates the standard by which all new information is measured, how can parents do their best to make sure they are the first ones to instruct their children about sex? (If the opportunity has already passed by with your older kids, Kris's material at www .moralrevolution.com might help you reestablish a healthy approach to the topic of sexuality with them.)

   _____

   _____

   _____

   _____

   _____

3. You read in RGK today about how Bill and Beni made a big event out of giving their children purity rings. In what way will you be intentional about setting an open, honest atmosphere where you can talk about sex with your children, as they did?

   _____

   _____

   _____

   _____

   _____

4. Given that today's culture often reinforces the lie that our sex drive defines or controls us, why is it so important to teach our children that we are not defined by our temptations?

_____

_____

_____

_____

_____

_____

Day 2

Safeguarding Unity

But did He not make them one, having a remnant of the Spirit?
And why one? He seeks godly offspring.

Malachi 2:15 NKJV

IN TODAY'S LESSON, you will read about the dating standards Beni and I set for our children. Even today, with all our kids grown and married, people still approach Beni about these standards to get her wisdom in this area. Our goal in setting standards was never to take the joy out of our kids' dating process, but rather to safeguard the unity of their eventual marriage. Again, it was more a matter of teaching them to say *yes* to the right thing, along with saying *no* to the wrong thing.

There is so much more to the depth of unity in marriage than a husband and wife coming together as one physically. Marriage is meant to shadow the much greater reality of Christ and His Bride, and our homes are meant to reflect the healthy environment known in heaven itself. When we put things in place to safeguard the unity of marriage, it highlights something eternally powerful to the world, and godly offspring are the result.

- Today's Scripture reading: Malachi 2:13–16; 1 Corinthians 10:14–22
- Today's reading from *Raising Giant-Killers*: the next few pages of chapter 13, from "The Purpose and Standards for Dating" through "The Act of Marriage"

Questions to Consider

1. What dating standards have you (or will you) put in place for your kids? If you adhered to similar standards when you were dating, share that testimony with your children. If you did not, what are some hard-learned lessons you could share that will help them adhere to godly standards from the start?

_____

_____

_____

_____

_____

2. How will you explain the purpose of dating to your children? Again, how is that similar to, or different from, the approach you took when you were dating, and what lessons did you learn that you can share with your kids?

_____

_____

_____

_____

_____

3. Do you think dating standards should change for an engaged couple? Why is premarital sex still wrong once they are headed for the altar? What are some ways that they can continue to safeguard the eventual unity of their marriage before they say "I do"?

_____

_____

_____

_____

_____

4. You will hear Bill make the statement in this session's video that immorality is a sin that is different from all other sins, in that sins have different consequences. In what way does an immoral sexual act violate the privilege of being one with Christ? In what way does sexual intercourse within the context of marriage illustrate that privilege?

Day 3

Rules from Love

For we must all appear before the judgment seat of Christ, so that each one may be recompensed for his deeds in the body, according to what he has done, whether good or bad.

2 Corinthians 5:10

HAVE YOU ESTABLISHED any "rules from love" or strict standards in your home that your children may think are unkind or unfair? Sometimes that is the reality of being an intentional parent. In the story about Highway 299 that I tell you in today's RGK reading, it was more important to me that my kids *lived* than that they liked or understood my rule about crossing the highway!

It goes without saying that intentional parents do all they can to protect the physical lives of their children. But parents who are raising giant-killers also do all they can to protect their children's minds and spirits. In our home, that meant I did not allow secular music, because I knew the effect it had had on me. You may choose to do differently in your home, but whatever you allow or disallow, monitor the resulting atmosphere and attitudes of your family. We each must ultimately give an account to God for the way we lived, and the way we keep each other accountable in our homes helps our children learn what He values.

- Today's Scripture reading: 2 Corinthians 5:1–11
- Today's reading from *Raising Giant-Killers*: the next few pages of chapter 13, from "Rules from Love" through "Shame and Design"

Questions to Consider

1. What "rules from love" do you have for your children? How do you handle it when they don't understand your rules or protest that the rules are unfair?

2. How have you been monitoring your family's listening and viewing habits to see that they are receiving from people whose imaginations are influenced by Kingdom values? If you have not been watchful in protecting your family from other people's ungodly imaginations, what will you do to start now?

3. Rather than allowing a lot of secular influence on your household and children, what steps could you take to focus your hearts on what you see the Lord blessing?

4. What does it mean to say that moral values are not externally imposed standards; they are an expression of conscience?

Day 4

Agreement Not Required

For they exchanged the truth of God for a lie, and worshiped
and served the creature rather than the Creator.

Romans 1:25

LOVING PEOPLE, regardless of their issues, is our number one as-
signment. You will read that same sentence again today in RGK,
because it is important. But it is equally important not to succumb
to the pressure of agreeing with what is wrong, that we might show
compassion. You will read that sentence again, too, because we must
never be willing to exchange the truth of God for a lie in the name of
compassion.

Our agreement is not required in order to love people we don't agree
with. Many well-meaning believers have difficulty making a distinction
between compassion and compromise, yet we can love people *and* disagree with them, without rejecting them.

The political climate of today would not agree with that, but it is true
all the same. And as you will learn in today's lesson, it is a vitally important principle to teach our children, many of whom face demonically
inspired issues like the gender "question" and homosexuality every day
in the school systems. We can teach our kids to love people well without
judgment *or* compromise. That kind of love is one of the hallmarks of
a giant-killer.

- Today's Scripture reading: Romans 1:18–32
- Today's reading from *Raising Giant-Killers*: the last few pages of
  chapter 13, starting at "Homosexuality"

Questions to Consider

1. As Bill said, Jesus is returning for a Bride, not a boyfriend. Yet every day, many of our kids will be exposed to others who are struggling with homosexuality or the concept of gender, in opposition to God's created design. What are some ways you can teach your children to offer compassion and prayer to such people, without agreeing with the underlying issues?

---

2. Why do you think so many believers today find it such a challenge to love with compassion, without agreeing with the point of view of the person being loved?

---

3. Why does "finding the gold" and speaking to that in people work so well in the context of situations where we disagree with them, but still want to love them and model the Kingdom? How will you teach your children to find the gold in others?

---

4. What is the result of raising our children to embrace God's design for sexuality?

Session 7 Video Takeaways

- God made healthy sexuality for procreation and pleasure.
- When God brings something into our life, the consequences are only joy and pleasure.
- The first person to address a subject with a child sets the standard of authority.
- The parent wants to be the one who introduces the subject of sex early on in a healthy, non-shameful way.
- We have to be wise when we expose ourselves to other people's imagination.
- When you protect purity, you pay a price to give a gift to your spouse on your wedding night.
- "We are not defined by our temptations." —Kris Vallotton
- Some of the Boundaries for Dating:
    1. Don't be alone in a home with a person of the opposite sex.
    2. Don't do anything that will arouse interest in a sexual experience.
- Immorality is a sin that is different than all other sins. Sins have different consequences.
- Immorality is a sin against your own body.
- God is the author of pleasure, and pleasure is best discovered by following design.
- Whenever you remove the concept of a Creator/the consciousness of a Designer, you no longer have design.
- Written into design is purpose.
- Purpose implies accountability.
- Every time we think outside of divine design, we violate why we are here.
- All beauty is defined by God's holiness.
- Holiness is setting things according to design; it is restoring things to purpose.
- If you remove design, you remove purpose, you remove accountability, you've undermined one of the most important elements in life: the fear of God.
- Jesus is not returning for a boyfriend. He's coming back for a Bride.
- We need to seriously pray into this great privilege that we have to help see people get restored to design.

Exposure to the Right Things

In the same way that children need seven positive comments to offset every one negative comment, so our children must be exposed to things that are right in contrast to the pain and needs of this world. If they are exposed only to need and tragedy, they will have little hope of changing it. But should they become anchored in their souls to the way of life that God intended, they will be less likely to cower in the face of insurmountable challenges. Promise, purpose and reward help bolster the hearts of those inclined to avoid such opportunities.

We are raising children not only to bring life and fix problems; we are raising a generation to be the solution to problems. We are instilling in them more than a skill set. The value system of God, established deep in our hearts, includes our access to His unlimited resources. Those resources enable us to be what is needed. As someone once said, "Don't try to be the best in the world. Try to be the best *for* the world."

Raising Giant-Killers, chapter 14

Day 1

The Concept of Exposure

For I was hungry, and you gave Me something to eat; I was thirsty, and you gave Me something to drink.

Matthew 25:35

W E ALL UNDERSTAND the danger of exposure to deadly things like radiation, and we would never purposely allow our children to be exposed to such things. In today's lesson, however, I ask you to take that familiar concept of exposure to something life-threatening and completely turn it around. What if there were things more powerful than radiation that had a *positive* effect on people? Then it would become life-giving to selectively expose our children to such things while they were young.

Beni and I were determined to expose our children to the right things early on. In RGK I go into more detail about what those things were and how we did it, but one of the main things was world need. We exposed our kids to people in various parts of the world who needed our compassion and help due to poverty, disease and hunger. We also exposed them to needs closer to home—people with immediate needs who crossed our path in our local community. We frequently involved our kids in serving people who could never pay us back, and we took them on mission trips and sent them for themselves once they were old enough.

Exposing your children firsthand to this world's need, particularly its need to hear the Gospel, exponentially multiplies the effects of anything you could say to them about it. The right kinds of exposure will literally change their lives.

- Today's Scripture reading: Matthew 25:31–40
- Today's reading from *Raising Giant-Killers*: the first half of chapter 14, through "Missions"

Questions to Consider

1. How does exposing children to other people's needs ward off the sense of entitlement that is so prevalent in our present day?

2. Compassion is the norm. What responses have you seen in your children that show how, by nature, God has designed them to be compassionate? What are some things you can do to give them the opportunity to act on their compassion?

3. The safety of the family is a parent's primary concern and responsibility. What are some ways you can think of to make sure the exposure of your children to need is age appropriate for them and takes place in safety?

4. Some great missionary statesmen have said, "The light that shines the farthest shines the brightest at home." How does that apply in the context of exposing our children to need?

Day 2

Pain, Purpose and Promises

And we know that God causes all things to work together for good to those who love God, to those who are called according to His purpose.

Romans 8:28

I HATE PAIN IN ANY FORM, but it does have its purposes. We are wise to learn how to use it to our advantage. One thing seeing pain does is cause compassion to rise in the hearts of our children. We talked about that in Day 1. Our kids saw tragedy firsthand when Beni and I took in some foster children, but they also saw the impact that God's love, expressed through our family, had on those children who were placed in our house of safety and refuge.

We taught our kids to confess and proclaim the promises of God in the midst of pain—theirs and other people's. Psychologists tell us that people who avoid pain often suffer mental illness as a result. A Kingdom lifestyle tells us that people who will trust in God's promises in the midst of pain find solutions as a result. In fact, such faith-filled people often *become* the solutions.

As you will hear me say in this session's video, a believer should be moved to compassion and bring a supernatural element into a person's life to heal and restore. That is one of the things we can help our young giant-killers learn to do in the face of this world's need and pain.

- Today's Scripture reading: 2 Samuel 24:18–25; Nehemiah 8:1–8
- Today's reading from *Raising Giant-Killers*: the second half of chapter 14, starting at "Foster Children"

Questions to Consider

1. No parent wants to see his or her child exposed to or experiencing pain, but what are some advantages to learning how to face pain in a healthy way?

   _____

   _____

   _____

   _____

2. Remember Bill's example in the book about urging Bethel parents to attend a Good Friday community service without childcare available? What Kingdom-oriented activities do you inconvenience yourself for, and what does that speak to your children?

   _____

   _____

   _____

   _____

3. What do you think it takes to anchor your children's souls to the way of life that God intended, so they will know they have access to His unlimited resources whenever they face a challenge or a need?

   _____

   _____

   _____

   _____

4. In this world we all face mystery, challenges, pain and need. Yet as Kris Vallotton says, "All things work for good in the end. If it's not good, it's not the end." What does that statement do to your heart? Share that with your young giant-killers the next time one of them is facing something difficult.

   _____

   _____

   _____

   _____

Day 3

Go Far, Go Together

So we, who are many, are one body in Christ, and individually members one of another.

Romans 12:5

I LIKE TO DEFINE FELLOWSHIP as *the exchange of life, from one member to another*. That exchange of life is what takes place when we are in community with other believers. One kind of positive exposure that will have lasting influence and bring life to our children (and to us) is exposure to community.

As the wonderful African proverb I quote in RGK says, *If you want to go fast, go alone. But if you want to go far, go together*. You and your children will grow stronger and go farther in community with others. And community starts at home. My parents modeled that for me when they invited my aunt and her household to move in with us after my uncle passed away. Beni and I modeled it for our children when we invited Kris and Kathy Vallotton to move in with us while they were building a home.

There are many ways to model the strength of community to our children, whether we open our home to another family at some point, or simply join a home group through our church. But one way or another, we owe exposure to the ongoing experience of community to our children.

- Today's Scripture reading: Romans 12:3–18
- Today's reading from *Raising Giant-Killers*: the first half of chapter 15, through "Life Together"

Questions to Consider

1. Those of us in the Western Church tend to emphasize our individual relationship with God over the corporate. If this has been true of you, what steps can you take to do a better job of exposing your children to the positive effects of community?

2. What does it mean to say that people are like gold mines? How does community help point to the rich vein of gold in every life?

3. We need people, and we need to teach our children how to develop meaningful relationships with people who will make them stronger and bring out the best in them. How do you balance time for solitude, or even family time, with the need for community?

4. In what ways do you think exposure to community can help develop your children's emotional intelligence (EI)? In what ways will that EI help them later in life?

Day 4

The Context of Community

Let us continually offer up a *sacrifice of praise* to God. . . . And do not neglect *doing good* and *sharing*, for with such sacrifices God is pleased.

Hebrews 13:15–16, emphasis added

IN TODAY'S LESSON we will talk about three New Testament sacrifices we are to make: praise, doing good and sharing. Among those three, sharing is "fellowship" in the original language of Scripture. It is the exchange of life one to another in the context of community. Exposing your children to community will cost you something in time and effort, but as you saw in Day 3, it is vital for their growth and strength (as well as for your own).

Today we will look at certain things that are best gained in the context of community. Provision is one of them. Community provides. Accountability is another. Community holds us to account for our God-given abilities and gifts. Maturity is a third. Community gives us a context for growth, an atmosphere in which we can learn and be lovingly corrected. There is no substitute for exposing your children to community. Don't neglect it!

- Today's Scripture reading: Hebrews 13:15–21
- Today's reading from *Raising Giant-Killers*: the second half of chapter 15, starting at "The Sacrifice"

Questions to Consider

1. Meaningful relationships cost us something. What kind of richness have you found in this kind of sacrifice? What can you teach your children about community through sharing with them about this?

   _____

   _____

   _____

   _____

2. What stories can you tell your children about having the opportunity to care for others in a practical way in community? What opportunities can you think of where you could involve them in doing the same?

   _____

   _____

   _____

   _____

3. Accountability does more than keep us from sin. In the context of community, how does it help us give an _account_ for our _ability_?

   _____

   _____

   _____

   _____

4. Why is it important, if we are not going to feel alone in a crowd, that we be willing to receive correction in the context of community?

   _____

   _____

   _____

   _____

Session 8 Video Takeaways

- Expose your children to human need (age appropriately).
- Through our lifestyle, we teach our children what we're willing to pay a price for.
- Traditions aren't evil unless they replace relationship.
- Expose your children to the value of community for traditions that prophesy and testify of what God values.
- Three things God considers to be a sacrifice:
  1. Thanksgiving and praise
  2. To do good
  3. Share/Fellowship
- The word *share* means "fellowship."
- One sacrifice is directed toward God. The other two are directed toward people.
- Every believer is a minister:
  1. To God
  2. To the Church
  3. To the world
- My ministry to God has an effect on how I minister to, love and value people.
- According to a psychologist, 90 percent of all mental illness is related to the attempt to avoid pain.
- Exposure to age-appropriate pain will equip your children with tools for communication, resolving conflict, addressing problems and reaching dreams.
- Expose your children to opportunity so that God can speak to and through them.
- In exposing your children to community, you expose them to a lifestyle of sowing into other people and also receiving.
- Give to things that you have no personal return for except in heaven.
- Expose your children to things you can't fix, because that helps to automatically nurture and develop their prayer life.
- Become as intentional as possible about exposing your children to need, because by nature God has designed them to be compassionate.

- A believer should be moved to compassion and bring a supernatural element into a person's life to heal and restore.
- "If you want to go fast, go alone. If you want to go far, go together." —African proverb.
- Include your children in the process, which will help them develop emotionally to respond to need out of health.

Exposure to the Supernatural

I guess it is a given for us to want our children to encounter God. I have fought specifically for my children to see and experience an authentic move of God through the years. If God was doing it, I wanted it for myself and for my family. I traveled when necessary and spent time with heroes of the faith whenever possible. It was a fundamental responsibility of mine to make sure that my household was exposed to the *more of God*.

We all have different kinds of opportunities in front of us. Some of them are major chances for significant change. Others are more subtle. If we take the ones God has given us, He will give us more, and the opportunities will grow in significance. You attract what you hunger for.

Raising Giant-Killers, chapter 16

Day 1

The Distinguishing Mark

Israel served the LORD all the days of Joshua and all the days of the elders who survived Joshua, and had known all the deeds of the LORD which He had done for Israel.

Joshua 24:31

WHEN IT COMES TO POSITIVE EXPOSURE, the bottom line is, I want my family exposed to God, the Great I AM, and I want them exposed to the Bible as God's Word. This whole ninth session, and the whole sixteenth chapter you are about to read in RGK, will focus exclusively on the bottom line of exposing our children to the supernatural.

Exposure to God and His works has been the distinguishing mark of great leaders throughout biblical history. It had an effect on them that could not be caught or taught any other way. The effect of such exposure does not show up on a leadership skills chart, but it is unmistakably there all the same. When you do all you can to expose your young giant-killers to the *more of God*, it will mark them for life.

- Today's Scripture reading: Joshua 24:14–31
- Today's reading from *Raising Giant-Killers*: the first few pages of chapter 16, through "The Distinguishing Mark"

Questions to Consider

1. What does it mean to say that you attract what you hunger for? How does that apply to exposing your children to the supernatural?

   _____

   _____

   _____

   _____

2. Why do you suppose it was twice repeated in Scripture that what distinguished Joshua and his leadership team was their exposure to the works of God? What does that signify for intentional parents?

   _____

   _____

   _____

   _____

3. In what ways was Joshua able to draw from a different resource in his leadership, simply because of what he had been exposed to in the supernatural? How have you found that to be true in your life, and how will you make sure it is true in your children's?

   _____

   _____

   _____

   _____

4. Look again in today's RGK reading at the five basic facts God's best leaders must live consciously aware of (under "The Distinguishing Mark" heading). Are you reinforcing these realities in the daily life of your household? How might you highlight them even more in your children's awareness?

   _____

   _____

   _____

   _____

Day 2

That Strange Tension

When Moses returned to the camp, his servant Joshua, the son of Nun, a young man, would not depart from the tent.

Exodus 33:11

A LOT OF PEOPLE make the supernatural spooky. It should not be. Beni and I worked hard to take the spookiness out of the supernatural for our kids. As I tell you in RGK today, we wanted God and His deeds to be part of our kids' normal experience, yet also remain awe-inspiring and amazing to them.

That is the strange tension we navigate as intentional parents—not making the supernatural seem distant or spooky, yet not making it seem so common or casual that it can be disregarded or disrespected. Although it takes a bit of balance sometimes, exposing your kids to the supernatural will be worth any time, money or risk it entails.

It is fantastic when a parent sees God move and then influences his or her children because of that exposure. But it is exponentially more powerful to have children see God move themselves. You will read about how our friends the prophets helped Beni and me expose our kids to God's work and His ways. Look around and pray for similar opportunities that will help you expose your children to the supernatural. Remember, you attract what you hunger for. If you will make it a priority, God will provide your family with powerful times in His presence.

- Today's Scripture reading: Exodus 33:7–11
- Today's reading from *Raising Giant-Killers*: the next few pages of chapter 16, from "The Effect of the Miraculous" through "Our Friends the Prophets"

Questions to Consider

1. What effects have your children shown already from being exposed to God and His supernatural interventions? Or if this is a new concept to you, what steps will you take from here out to expose your children to the *more of God*?

   _____

   _____

   _____

   _____

   _____

   _____

2. Today's culture exposes many children to the spooky part of the supernatural that has nothing to do with God and His works. What will you teach your children to do when one of their friends brings up that kind of experience?

   _____

   _____

   _____

   _____

   _____

   _____

3. Have you experienced places where the supernatural was made to seem so aloof and distant that nobody could approach it? What about the opposite scenario, where it is made to seem so casual that it is disregarded or disrespected? How will you balance that strange tension with your children?

   _____

   _____

   _____

   _____

   _____

4. Who are the people in your life who see the treasure in your kids and call it out, as Bill related that his friends Dick Mills and Dick Joyce did for his family? If that has never taken place, who are some people with that potential whom you could invite into your home for a meal and some fellowship around the table with you and your children?

_____

_____

_____

_____

_____

_____

Day 3

A Place of Sacrifice

You also are being built together into a dwelling of God in the Spirit.

Ephesians 2:22

Your schedule reveals your priorities. Your schedule reveals what you hunger for. So does mine. Certainly, there have always been things I have attended as a Church leader as part of the job. Yet there have also been all kinds of things I have attended because I hungered for the *more of God*, not because I was required to be there. Sometimes it was a sacrifice, even for my family, but it was always worth it.

How about you? Do you keep your schedule convenient and easy, or do you live in a place of sacrifice? Sacrifice is what it takes if we want our children to see the value we put on divine encounters with the God of all might and power. As I say in today's reading, there are some things you will only find in the corporate gathering. When your family is in such a meeting and the fire falls on your sacrifice, it will change you all for the long haul.

- Today's Scripture reading: 1 Corinthians 15:1–8; Ephesians 2:19–22
- Today's reading from *Raising Giant-Killers*: the next few pages of chapter 16, from "Not a Perfect Schedule" through "Lifelong Indebtedness"

Questions to Consider

1. What kind of value did your parents place on corporate church gatherings when you were growing up (if any at all)? How did that affect you positively or negatively? In what way is your value for those gatherings increasing as you work through this session?

   _____

   _____

   _____

   _____

2. What do we owe our children beyond family devotions and being a good Christian example? Why is this so important to think about?

   _____

   _____

   _____

   _____

3. *Most of what you need in life will be brought to you. But most of what you want, you'll have to go get.* What application does this statement of Bill's have spiritually for you and your family, and what will you do about it?

   _____

   _____

   _____

   _____

4. In what way have you experienced the tension between resting and fighting, between receiving and apprehending, and between living as a child of God and living as a responsible soldier of Christ? What will you teach your children about navigating this?

   _____

   _____

   _____

   _____

Day 4

Wise Parents Travel

And let us consider how to stimulate one another to love and good deeds, not forsaking our own assembling together, as is the habit of some, but encouraging one another; and all the more as you see the day drawing near.

Hebrews 10:24–25

TODAY IN RGK, I tell you about more than one move of God I have experienced, often with my children present. Having my children there at such times has had a profound effect on them, as we have been talking about all through this session. I also tell you about watching children at our church experience and enjoy the manifestations of God and thinking to myself, *Maybe I should follow them.*

It is so important not only for our kids to see people doing God's work, but for them actually *to see God at work.* Wise men—wise, intentional parents—still travel to make sure that happens. And they send their kids to see Him work in various places, once the kids are age appropriate. Now I even send my grandkids, because when exposure to the supernatural is passed from generation to generation, a legacy of giant-killers is the result.

- Today's Scripture reading: Hebrews 10:19–25
- Today's reading from *Raising Giant-Killers*: the last few pages of chapter 16, starting at "Our Own Move of God"

Questions to Consider

1. Exposure, exposure, experience, experience. We cannot force our children to experience anything supernatural, but we can make them hungry and available. How can you foster that exposure and experience more in your children?

----

2. Are your kids mostly seeing people do God's work, or have you put them in environments where they are actually *seeing God work*? What is the long-term effect of making sure they see both?

----

3. Bill told you in RGK about some of the different people and ministries he has made sure to expose his children and now grandchildren to, even when he and his family had to travel to make it happen. In what ways are you exposing your family to those who function differently in the Holy Spirit than you do? Why is that of extreme importance?

----

4. What kind of mission trip or other trip have you considered taking your family on? What kinds of plans are you putting in place to carry it out?

Session 9 Video Takeaways

- Expose your children to what God says about them.
- We want to connect our children to God's dream.
- God gives us dreams that require two things:
  1. His supernatural activity
  2. Our need for people.
- The stories of the supernatural are available to all of us.
- "Children don't receive a junior Holy Spirit." —Dick Joyce
- We choose our moments well to expose our children to certain things.
- Expose your children to the giftings of other people.
- Wise men still travel.
- If it's in your heart and you create room for it, God will pour into it.
- Choose to expose yourself to the supernatural things you want to see in your life.
- Discipline is important for our personal transformation, but the greatest change comes as we are exposed to His glory.
- As parents, you want to do everything you can to teach your children to stay in that moment of God's presence and power.
- Don't underestimate what children can receive in a given meeting.
- There is impact simply because they're in a room where God is manifested as God.

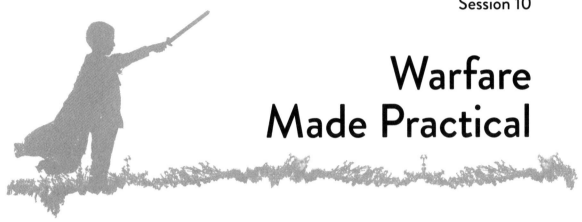

Warfare Made Practical

God has chosen our families to have an impact on the course of world history. We have been given all the tools we need to bring about the transformation and discipleship of nations that He longs for. Everything we will ever need was provided for us in the sacrifice of the Lamb of God on our behalf. And it is from the place of His accomplishment that we have the confidence to live, serve and envision the future. For this reason, we have unfailing hope.

This is what Jesus paid for. He longs for us to have children, who have children, who have children . . . who will impact the world with His love, power, wisdom and purity. And it is to this end that we embrace the privilege of *intentional parenting*—raising giant-killers!

Raising Giant-Killers, chapter 17

Day 1

Four Weapons for Giant-Killers

In accordance with the prophecies previously made concerning
you . . . fight the good fight.

1 Timothy 1:18

BACK AT THE VERY BEGINNING, in Day 1 of Session 1, we talked about how we are all born into a war. And while I have never lived overly devil conscious, I did try to teach my children about the devil's devices and how to win any battle he wages. That is why in today's RGK reading, I tell you the story about the terrors in the night Brian used to experience as a child and what we did about them. In the depths of the night, I taught Brian how to wage spiritual warfare using four weapons that would enable him to live a victorious lifestyle. You can teach your young giant-killers in training how to use these same weapons, which we will look at today:

1. The blood of Jesus
2. The Word of God
3. The name of Jesus
4. Praise

Really, we all need these four weapons, but our young giant-killers especially need to learn how to use them for themselves. It is the "give a man a fish versus teaching him to fish" idea. Either our kids can depend on others to help them be okay, or they can practice their proficiency with these tools until they can employ them to overcome the enemy.

Brian learned to fight with them and win. If you teach your kids how to wield these same spiritual weapons, they will do likewise.

- Today's Scripture reading: Psalm 68:1–4; Proverbs 18:10; Isaiah 42:1–13
- Today's reading from *Raising Giant-Killers*: the first half of chapter 17, through "The Battleground Called Night"

Questions to Consider

1. You will hear Bill say in this session's video that when we have to go through a fight to step into something, we gain authority in that area. That happened with Brian as his personal victory over night terrors became a corporate blessing through which he has now led countless people into freedom. Think of some areas in which you need to help your children gain their own personal victories. Why is that more productive than fixing everything for them?

   _____

   _____

   _____

   _____

2. How will you help your children practice using the four weapons for giant-killers? And before you answer that, are you employing these four weapons for yourself? The more your battle skills stay sharp, the better you can teach the young giant-killers in training who are under your care.

   _____

   _____

   _____

   _____

3. It took Brian some time to gain his victory. But anytime there is a long-term battle in an area, the Lord is using that to build in us the clarity of heart and mind to know our authority and our identity. What has He built in you through some of the long-term battles you have experienced? Have you shared that with your children to encourage them?

   _____

   _____

   _____

   _____

4. What does it mean to say that God uses the devil's strategy against him by making the targeted area of weakness in us into a new area of strength?

_____

_____

_____

_____

_____

Day 2

Victory in the Home

But as for me and my house, we will serve the LORD.
Joshua 24:15

TODAY WE LOOK MORE CLOSELY at one of the four weapons we covered in Day 1, the blood of Jesus. This time, though, we consider it as it is found in the Eucharist—Communion. We will also look at the bread, His broken body. For Beni and me, Communion is a special time in which we give the Lord honor and praise for His priceless work. It has also become a primary tool of our lives for the sake of our family. It can become the same for you. You will read today about how I take Communion while covering each of my family members in prayer.

You will also read about three specific ways the power of God/will of God is released through us. These ways are through a *decree*, the *act of faith* and a *prophetic act*. I urge you as an intentional parent to try these things at home. Each of these actions can become a tool that helps bring about breakthrough in your family life. Breakthroughs of promise follow our sacrificial parenting, just as resurrection followed the cross. Jesus' victory from the grave becomes our victory in the home.

- Today's Scripture reading: 2 Kings 6:1–7; 1 Peter 2:21–25
- Today's reading from *Raising Giant-Killers*: the second half of chapter 17, starting at "The Table of the Lord"

Questions to Consider

1. When, where and how often do you partake of Communion? For the sake of your family, after today's lesson what will you change about your approach?

_____

_____

_____

_____

_____

2. Look again in today's RGK reading (under "The Blood" heading) at the list of the very specific things Bill prays during Communion that cover each family member. What would a similar list be that you could begin to pray specifically for your family when you take Communion? Are there other people you would also include praying for during that time, as Bill does?

_____

_____

_____

_____

_____

3. Some things just need to be said. Jesus spoke with authority to the issues He faced. Do you make a point of releasing the power of God/will of God over your household through decrees? Write some decrees here, and then speak them out. There is life in the power of your tongue.

_____

_____

_____

_____

_____

4. Is there anything the Holy Spirit has been directing you to do that seems unreasonable (an act of faith), or that seems to have no logical connection to your desired outcome in a situation (a prophetic act)? Grab the moment and follow that direction, which is a great way to teach your young giant-killers about using their Kingdom authority here on the earth.

_____

_____

_____

_____

_____

_____

Day 3

Three Special Additions

A pupil is not above his teacher; but everyone, after he has been fully trained, will be like his teacher.

Luke 6:40

THERE WERE FOUR SPECIAL THINGS I thought were important to share about raising giant-killers that I did not write into the chapter text of *Raising Giant-Killers*. I made each of them into an appendix at the back of the book for you instead, and I don't want you to miss them. Today let's look at the first three, and in Day 4 we will look at the fourth and final one.

Appendix 1 in RGK is a letter I wrote to my son Eric in June 1994 that addressed the 10 things I wanted my children to know before they left home. These 10 things applied to Brian and Leah as well, and they were my goals for *intentional parenting*.

Appendix 2 details a pattern for Sunday school we adopted over three decades ago that is timeless and is still excellent to put to use today. The pattern focuses on sharing love, understanding God's truth, exploring His Word and applying what you know as a family. You will find this pattern a useful foundation to build on with your children.

Appendix 3 is a declaration written by people who serve in our church's children's ministry. They based this declaration around my teaching on the four cornerstones of thought, which you read about back in chapter 3 of the book. Making this declaration with your children as a confession is a practical way to imbed these vital cornerstones deep into your children's hearts—as well as into your own.

- Today's Scripture reading: John 1:9–18
- Today's reading from *Raising Giant-Killers*: appendix 1, appendix 2 and appendix 3

Questions to Consider

1. What are the top things you want your children to know before leaving home? Some of yours may be the same as Bill's top 10 things, but make a note here of any additional ones that are also important to you.

   _____

   _____

   _____

   _____

   _____

2. When Eric was old enough, Bill gave him the letter you just read of the top 10 things he wanted his son to know before leaving home. How will you express to your children the things you believe are the most important for them to know before they leave your daily parental oversight and teaching?

   _____

   _____

   _____

   _____

   _____

3. Are you in the habit of doing a home Sunday school or devotion-type of activity with your children (and perhaps their friends)? What did you glean from the appendix 2 parent's guide that might work well in your household?

   _____

   _____

   _____

   _____

   _____

4. What does it do to your heart when you make the declaration Bill shared with you in appendix 3? What are some ways that you could make this and similar declarations part of your regular routine in raising your giant-killers?

_____

_____

_____

_____

_____

_____

Day 4

Praying the Bible

All your children shall be taught by the Lord, and great shall be the peace of your children.

Isaiah 54:13 NKJV

IN APPENDIX 4 OF RGK, you will find a fourth and final, indescribably powerful tool that I want to leave you with as you parent with divine purpose to raise giant-killers. As I said back in chapter 10 of the book, when we pray the Bible—combining the beauty of Scripture with the privilege of prayer—it creates a beautiful rainbow of hope and protection over our children.

My mother was and is a giant herself in this respect. She has prayed the verses in appendix 4 for years over her children, grandchildren and now even great-grandchildren. The list is hers, and she gave it to all the parents in our family to empower us in our intentional parenting. Now I pass it on to you so you can pray these passages, too.

Treasure your children as the gift from God that they are, celebrate them as a reward from Him and pray the Bible over them continuously. As you do these things, you will see them transform into powerful weapons of war. You will also leave as your legacy generations of giant-killers who know how to live the lifestyle of the Kingdom that proclaims of our Lord, "Your kingdom come. Your will be done, on earth as it is in heaven."

- Today's Scripture reading: the passages you will find in appendix 4
- Today's reading from *Raising Giant-Killers*: appendix 4

Questions to Consider

1. Do you have a legacy in your family line of the parents praying the Bible over the children? If so, wonderful! Continue it with divine purpose and power. What effect can you see that it has had on your life, and now on the lives of your children? (If you do not have such a legacy, see question 2.)

_____

_____

_____

_____

_____

2. If you do not have such a legacy in your family line, be the first to start the practice of praying the Bible over your children. Using appendix 4, choose two or three passages that stand out to you as ones you most need to pray over your children and note them here. Then begin the privilege of praying God's heart over your kids.

_____

_____

_____

_____

_____

3. Are there any passages of Scripture you already pray over your children that you do not see included in appendix 4? Note them here, and pencil them into the appendix in the book if you will be using that as a reference for prayer.

_____

_____

_____

_____

_____

4. Who are the other parents among your family and friends who would benefit from a list of Scriptures so they can pray the Bible over their children? Make a list of the passages you pray, as Bill's mother did, and share it with them.

Session 10 Video Takeaways

- Don't emphasize an awareness of the devil, but also don't be ignorant of the devil or his devices.
- God has given us four weapons:
  1. The blood of Jesus
  2. The Word of God
  3. The name of Jesus
  4. Praise
- Declare over your family that the blood of Jesus sets them free.
- The blood of Jesus terrifies the enemy.
- Anytime there is a long-term battle in an area, the Lord is using that to build in us the clarity of heart and mind to know our authority and our identity.
- You don't want to fix everything for your children. Give them the opportunity to get their own personal victories.
- When we have to go through a fight to step into something, we gain authority in that area.
- One of the most important things we can impart to our kids is that we are absolutely dependent on hearing from God.
- What you want to do is stay in communication with your children as they are going through something.
- Keep your children from being introspective. The answer isn't inside; it's Him—the Lord Jesus Himself.
- God has appointed you as the authority over your children.
- In Communion, the bread is a testimony of His New Covenant in divine health.
- Implement through decree the power of God's divine Covenant.
- It was always God's intent that salvation visit entire households.
- God's desire is for a family line to gain in maturity and in gifting to express and reveal what He's like more clearly in the earth. (And you get that through multiple generations serving God.)
- Pray for people who have opposed you to be blessed and prosper.
- Don't come before God to criticize one of His kids.
- Things happen in the Kingdom through:
  1. Decree
  2. An act of faith

3. A prophetic act

- In this lifestyle of warfare, we have as parents a sacred role to raise up our children to make a difference in the world.

- Say yes to raising your children and your grandchildren intentionally, to raise them to be giant-killers.

RGK Q&A

Optional Wrap-Up

FROM THE EDITORS of Chosen Books: If your *Raising Giant-Killers* study group is meeting for this Session 11 optional wrap-up, note that there are no daily readings you need to do or questions you need to answer in preparation for your final session. You should now be finished reading the RGK book and should have completed this participant's guide. You may want to review this study's main points briefly and bring along any final questions you have for discussion. You may also want to have in mind a testimony you can share with your group about how this study has already helped you parent intentionally and with divine purpose. Talk to your group leader(s) for more details about what this final meeting will involve.

At the wrap-up meeting, your group will want to view the bonus Q&A video Bill recorded, which is about the same length as the other RGK videos you have seen already. In it, he addresses some excellent questions his video audience asks about intentional parenting. You will find the questions and answers interesting and informative.

If you are studying RGK on your own without the videos, or if your group meetings do not include viewing the bonus video, you can still benefit from the information Bill presents in the Q&A segment. The final video takeaways that follow are the questions he was asked, along with a summary of his answers.

RGK Q&A Video Takeaways

Question: *How do you raise confident young people who can be giant-killers, but at the same time not be prideful and self-centered?*
Answer:

- Refuse to be impressed with the size of the problem. Refuse to be impressed with the impact of culture.
- Expose your children to opportunities to sacrifice.
- Speak to what already exists in the child, that God has put there.
- The whole cycle of price and reward is a huge part of our faith.

Question: *What is a good age to talk to your children about sexual relations, and how do you go about that?*
Answer:

- What you say will develop over the years, as they have greater capacity to understand.
- Talk to them about what they can handle age appropriately.
- Start young, so it's an open subject from then on.

Question: *What would you say to parents who have the extra challenge of having a special needs kid about using these principles in the home?*
Answer:

- Get help as often as you need it.
- Always contend for the miracle (it comes in two ways—instant, and gradual).
- Lay hands on your children while they are sleeping.
- Find a word from God to declare over your children.

Question: *Could you share some thoughts or give advice on parenting your children through parenting, as they become parents? What does that relationship look like?*
Answer:

- When they become adults they're on their own, but you're still a parent. Don't try to regain control.
- Have faith in God's ability to work in and through them.
- As a grandparent you have a role, but your children are appointed by God to raise their children.

Question: *As parents of older children, getting this new perspective on things like discipline, how do you right the ship? How do you make that about-face?*

Answer:

- You serve a Father who is able to restore things back to better than they were before.
- One of the most important traits of a parent is humility (because you model how life works in the Kingdom).
- Pray, knowing that only God can make up for what they didn't get and give it to them now.

Question: *How should we intervene in difficult situations like unforgiveness between our kids?*

Answer:

- You can never force heart issues with your children.
- Pray that the Lord would deal with them, and then bring it up again later.
- Expose your children to the Scripture.

Question: *As a single parent, how do you ensure that you're walking your child through any healing necessary in cases where there's an absent parent?*

Answer:

- Pray over the child, especially when they're sleeping. Pray against trauma.
- As situations arise, ask God with your children to make up for what they are missing.
- There's always something missing, but our Father is big enough to more than make up for what is missing.
- Confess what you believe God will do for your children. Keep bringing them back to what Jesus has promised.

Question: *Some children tend to have a little more sensitivity to spiritual things, and it seems like at a young age they're bearing the weight of that and not experiencing the gift of that. How do you parent a child*

into that, to help them manage the responsibility, but also give them the ability to celebrate that gift?
Answer:

- Pray with your children that God will show them what He's doing.
- Stay open. Ask questions. Draw them into a place where you can pray together.
- The Lord will enable your children to harness that gift to be used proactively.
- You never react; you never deny. You listen, but always try to direct it into something that God is doing.

Question: *How do you handle lying? At a certain young age it seems almost like creative thinking! How do you instill a value for the truth?*
Answer:

- You can't shame a child into change.
- When the heat of the moment is gone, talk about the concept of and the importance of truth.
- Truth is solid. Lies are fractures in relationships.
- Expose your children to how God thinks. He really values truth. Truth sets free.

Question: *I wanted to ask about blended families, especially when you have a child who's influenced by different households.*
Answer:

- There's such uniqueness that each household can bring.
- Often an outcome is determined by your approach.
- When we are proactive, we come in responsively, not reactively.

Bill and Beni Johnson are the senior leaders of Bethel Church in Redding, California. Bill is a fifth-generation pastor with a rich heritage in the Holy Spirit. The present move of God has brought him into a deeper understanding of the phrase "on earth as it is in heaven." Heaven is the model for our life and ministry. Bill and the Bethel Church family have taken on this theme for life and ministry, where healing and miracles are normal. He teaches that we owe the world an encounter with God, and that a gospel without power is not the Gospel Jesus preached. Bill is also the co-founder of Bethel School of Supernatural Ministry (BSSM).

Beni is a pastor, author and speaker. She has a call to joyful intercession that is an integral part of Bethel Church. Her insight into strategies for prayer and her involvement in prayer networks bring breakthrough with global impact. She is passionate about health and wholeness—in body, soul and spirit.

Together, Bill and Beni serve a growing number of churches that have partnered for revival. This apostolic network has crossed denominational lines in building relationships that enable church leaders to walk in both purity and power. And as Bill says, home is the beginning point for having that kind of worldwide impact: "Success at home gives us the authority base to go anywhere else . . . it starts at home."

Bill and Beni's goal at home has always been to raise giant-killers through intentional parenting. Their three children are now married and are all serving with their spouses in full-time ministry. Between them, they have given Bill and Beni ten grandchildren who are also being raised as giant-killers.

Additional Notes

Additional Notes